About the author

Karen Thornton is currently a peripatetic teacher with the Birmingham Music Service, teaching flute, clarinet and saxophone. She also conducts the Birmingham Schools' Training Wind Orchestra. She gained a first class graduate diploma in jazz and contemporary music at the City of Leeds College of Music and has a postgraduate certificate from Trinity College of Music, Birmingham Conservatoire and the Open University. Karen plays with the Oasis Trio and the Danny Steel Orchestra, who perform regularly around the West Midlands.

The Questions
Dictionary of
MUSIC

Karen Thornton

The Questions Publishing Company Ltd

Birmingham

2000

©2000 The Questions Publishing Company
27 Frederick Street
Birmingham B1 3HH
Tel: 0121-212 0919
Fax: 0121-212 0959
url: www.education-quest.com

ISBN: 1 898149 85 2

Edited by Brian Asbury
Designed by Al Stewart
Illustrations by Sarah Hedley

Printed in Great Britain

Introduction

All areas of knowledge require at least some specialist language. The language of music can be especially difficult for children, as many of the words in its conventional vocabulary are non-English in origin. In addition to many special words, the language of music also includes many familiar-seeming words which have adopted a special meaning in this particular context (e.g. bridge, key, score), and this can be a source of confusion for children. If you have ever grappled with the problems of trying to guide pupils had through the often bewildering maze of music terminology, you may have wished there was an easy to understand reference book, written especially for pupils, to make it all clearer for them. If so, then wish no more: the book you hold in your hand is the answer you have been searching for.

However, this Music Dictionary is not just a list of words and their meanings. Its purpose is not only to help children understand the meaning of the words associated with music and to use them correctly: many entries also list examples of suggested listening so that they can hear for themselves what is described in the text.

Using the Music Dictionary

The best way to use this dictionary is to make it available in the class-room for children to use, either independently or together with the teacher, as the circumstances require. It can be presented as a book, or alternatively individual entries can be photocopied and fixed to A5 cards. However you opt to use it, the dictionary will provide an extra opportunity for children to extend their knowledge and understanding of music while also developing their reference skills.

It is an ideal medium for browsing during odd moments, giving chil-dren the opportunity to meet new ideas and information in a friendly and accessible format. If they encounter a word connected with music that they are not sure about or don't understand, they can look up what it means. Or they could pick out any word and find out more about it. This can help children to understand better what they already know, or to learn about something new.

Each word in this dictionary is explained in full (not just defined), and illustrations are used to help give it meaning and sense. Many of the words are related to each other.

Where a word is highlighted in individual entries in **bold**, this shows that it is defined elsewhere in the dictionary. Words used in music sometimes also have more than one meaning, and where possible all the different meanings of terms have been listed in each entry.

Symbols

Learning the language of music can be very enjoyable when it is expe-rienced in the right way. Wherever possible, the entries in this book have been presented in a manner that is fun as well as informative. Extensive use is made of examples and diagrams to illustrate the ideas that the words represent.

At the beginning of each entry is a symbol which shows what kind of word is being defined. You will find examples of each of these in this dictionary, and these symbols show what they are. There are four different symbols:

Elements of music

The concepts or 'building blocks' from which music is made – this covers words such as tempo, pitch, note and beat.

Musical styles

The different ways and techniques of playing music.

Music makers

The people who create and make music and the things which are used to make music – usually musical instruments.

Musical notation

This category includes a whole host of specialist words used in written music, from describing different kinds of notes to instructing players what kind of tempo to use.

Parents

Parents who are unfamiliar with the language of music, or those who have not studied music for some time, will find this dictionary helpful in:

✳ refreshing their memory.
✳ learning previously unfamiliar words and ideas of music.
✳ as a general reference.

It may even help them to help their children with homework.

Dictionary Entries

A capella

When vocal music is sung without any instrumental **accompaniment** it is called **a capella**.

The direct translation from Italian to English is 'in the church style', which is where it originated. A capella singing has since become an integral part of all styles of music. Barbershop **choirs** use this technique extensively.

Suggested listening:
Manhattan Transfer

Accent

When a **note** is played with more immediate force than other notes it is said to be **accented**. On **stave notation** an accent is signified by a small arrow above or below the given note.

Suggested listening:
Stravinsky, *The Rite of Spring*

Acciaccatura

An **acciaccatura** is a short crushed **note** which, when played, is squeezed in before the principal note. It is usually printed in a fainter print than the rest of the music. It gives the effect of almost 'tripping up' on a note.

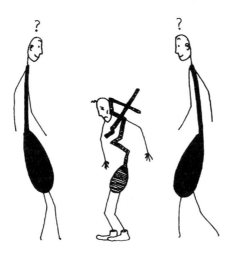

Suggested listening:
Prokoviev, *Peter and the Wolf* (flute part representing the bird)

Accidental

A **composer** who wishes to change the **pitch** of a **note** out of the given **key** signature will use an **accidental**. This can be by means of a *flat* sign ♭, which lowers the pitch of a note by a semitone, a *sharp* sign ♯, which raises the pitch by a semitone, or a *natural* sign ♮ which will resume a note to its original pitch.

Accompaniment

The music that backs up or supports an instrumental player or singer is called the **accompaniment**. This can range in form from a **piano** supporting the line of a soloist to a **string quartet** playing with a **rock** band.

Acoustics

The way that sound behaves in a given environment is described as the **acoustics**. This includes how much **echo** is apparent or how quickly music or sound starts and stops.

Acoustics will vary depending on the size of a room, what materials the walls are made of and what there is in the room for the sound to bounce off. For example, the acoustics of a church will allow the sound to bounce quite easily from the walls, and due to the high ceiling will create an echo. A bedroom, however, will probably be full of furniture and have carpet on the floor – all of which absorb sound and do not let it reverberate.

Adagio

Adagio is an Italian **tempo** (speed) marking which directs the piece to be played slowly. It will appear at the beginning of the piece or where the **composer** wishes to change the speed. The term can also be used as the title of a piece of music.

Suggested listening:
Barber's *Adagio for Strings*

Ad lib

A **composer** who wishes to allow a performer to use his or her discretion as how to play a section or how many times to play a section of music may write the word **ad lib**. (Ad lib is an abbreviation of the Latin *ad libitem*, which means according to pleasure.)

For example, a **drummer** in a **jazz band** may be given a direction at the beginning of a piece of music to play a given **rhythm** and then told to ad lib. The drummer would then continue the piece using his or her own ideas based on the pre-set ideas.

Allegro

Allegro is an Italian **tempo** (speed) marking meaning that the piece of music or section should be played in a merry, quick, lively and bright way.

Andante

Andante is an Italian **tempo** (speed) marking which means a piece of music or section should be played at walking pace.

The word andante is also often used as a title for a **composition**.

Anthem

An **anthem** is an English choral work which was originally intended to be sung in church services.

Each country of the world has a national anthem. The English National Anthem is *God Save the Queen*, which is sung on patriotic occasions. Anthems can also be considered as songs representative of special or memorable occasions. For example, *Three Lions* could be thought of as the Euro 1996 football anthem for England.

Appoggiatura

An **appoggiatura** is a **note** which is usually a step above or below the main note which has the effect of making the music **harmony** sound temporarily crushed. As it is a note which is taken from outside the **chord**, the appoggiatura is often written smaller and in a lighter type than the rest of the piece.

An appoggiatura will often take half the value of the main note, and performers will have to change the performance values themselves.

Aria

An **aria** is a **song** for **solo voice** which is accompanied by an **orchestra**. It is usually part of a bigger work such as an **opera**.

Suggested listening:
Giordani, *Caro mio ben*
Pergolesi, *Se tu M'ami, se sospiri*

Arpeggio

When the **notes** of a common **chord** are played in order, one after the other, this is called an **arpeggio**. The *first*, *third*, *fifth* and **octave** notes of a **scale** are used for an arpeggio.

If you can imagine a scale going up and down like a staircase, the arpeggio would be like going up and down but not using all the stairs.

Articulation

When someone talks very clearly and you can understand every word they say, they are said to have good **articulation**. In music, the method in which a **note** is produced on an **instrument** is called articulation. There are two main types of musical articulation – *staccato* and *legato*.

Staccato is when a note is played short and detached and is shown on musical **notation** as a small dot above or below the note.

Legato is when the note or **phrase** is played smoothly and is shown on music as a curved line.

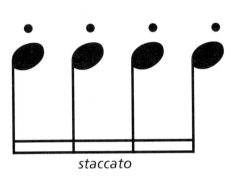

staccato

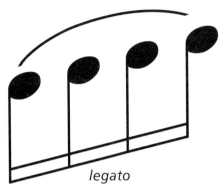

legato

Auxiliary notes

The type of **note** decoration which passes back to the note it has just left is called an **auxiliary** note.

For example: A *shake* or *trill* is the rapid movement from one note to the one above.

A *mordent* is a quick move from the given note to the one above and back

A *turn* travels from the note to the one above, back to the note, to the one below and finally back on the note.

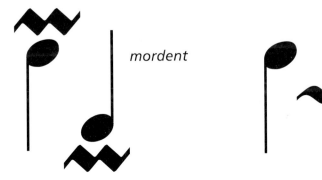

mordent

turn

Bagpipes

The traditional Scottish **bagpipes** date back to the 18th Century. They consist of a *bag* which is filled with air (by blowing through a pipe or by a pumping action from the arm), three *pipes* and a *finger tube*. As the bag is filled, air travels through the three pipes to create a **drone**, and by moving fingers over the finger tube the player creates a variety of **notes**.

Due to their penetrating sound, bagpipes lend themselves well to be being played outdoors.

Suggested listening:
Wings, *Mull of Kintyre*

Ballad

Traditionally a **ballad** was a **song** that could be danced to.

Throughout history it became a term to describe anything that could be sung, and today it describes a slow love song.

Suggested listening:
Beatles, *Yesterday*

Band

A group of instrumentalists is commonly called a **band**. Today the most common use of the word is used to describe a group of musicians who play **pop music**. It can involve any combination of musical **instruments**. Bands have been in existence since the Middle Ages, when town (wind) players came together to play.

There are now many forms of bands which join a designated group of instruments together. For example, a **brass** band is exclusively for instruments from the brass family – though latterly brass bands have also incorporated **percussion** instruments.

The predecessor to the pop band was the **jazz** band, which used instrumentalists plus a **rhythm** section – **bass**, **guitar** and **drums**. Larger jazz groups ('big bands') were introduced in the1930s.

Bar

A section of **stave notation** signified by a vertical line (bar line) is called a **bar**. When the **time signature** is 4/4 there will be four **crotchet beats** per bar.

The reason bars are used is to make reading the line of music easier and give it defined direction.

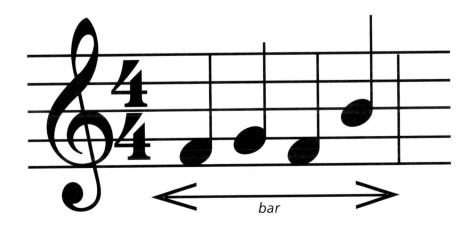

bar

Baroque

The era of music written between 1600 and 1750 is referred to as the **Baroque** era. The style of music differed from previous styles mainly due to the contrasts introduced, such as elaborate **ornamentation**.

The **organ** and **harpsichord** are prominent **instruments** in Baroque music.

Suggested listening:
J S Bach, *Brandenburg Concertos*
Vivaldi, *The Four Seasons*

Bass

1. **Bass** is a word used to describe the deepest **pitch** of the male **voice,** or any musical instrument or music to be played which is pitched in this range.

2. **Bass guitar** is the common name for the lowest pitched of the electric guitars. This usually has four **strings** (though has been known to have five). It is used a great deal in **pop bands**, though rarely as a **solo instrument**.

3. Another name for a **double bass**.

Suggested listening:
Jaco Pastorias

Bassoon

The **bassoon** is a **woodwind instrument**. The large wooden conical tube is played through a double **reed** via a small metal tube called a *crook*. The instrument has four sections: *bell*, *wing joint*, *long joint* and *butt*. Finger holes and **keys** are covered or pushed down to change **notes**.

The bassoon is considered the **bass** instrument of the **woodwind** family, though a *double bassoon*, which is larger and **pitched** an **octave** lower, is sometimes used.

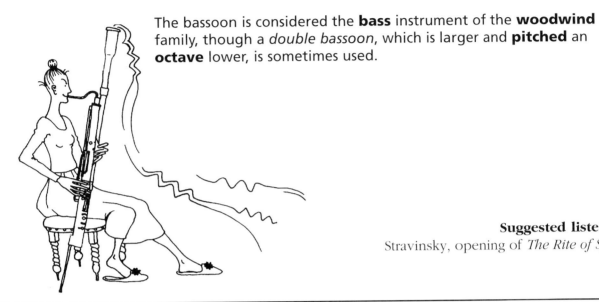

Suggested listening:
Stravinsky, opening of *The Rite of Spring*

Beat

The basic *pulse* which underlines most music is called the **beat**. When you listen to a piece of music and tap your foot, it is the beat you tap out.

Blues

The **blues** were traditionally folk based songs sung by black slaves working in the cotton fields of the southern states of the USA. With the introduction of instruments and Western **harmony** the *12-bar blues* evolved. As with all musical developments, the structure of the blues has changed and evolved over time, though the basic characteristics have remained the same even to this day.

Suggested listening:
Robert Johnson, *At the Crossroads*
Eric Clapton, *From the Cradle to the Grave*

Brass

1. The section of an **orchestra** consisting of **trumpet, trombone, tuba** and French **horn** is referred to as the **brass** section. All these **instruments** are made from brass and the sound is made by blowing through a *mouthpiece* while making the lips 'buzz'.

2. The section of a modern **band** which represents the **acoustic** blown **instruments** is called the **brass** section. This will often consist of a **saxophone, trumpet** and **trombone**.

Suggested listening:
The Grimethorpe Colliery Band
Earth, Wind and Fire

Bridge

1. A section of music which links passages together is known as a **bridge**.

2. The part of a stringed **instrument** over which the **strings** pass is known as the **bridge**.

bridge

Cadence

When music conventionally comes to the end of a section, **phrase** or piece, the formation of **chords** is called a **cadence**.

There are four widely used cadences: *Perfect*, when the fifth chord passes to the first (or *tonic*) chord and is commonly found at the end of a piece; *Interrupted*, when the fifth chord is followed by the sixth; *Imperfect* when the first chord is followed by the fifth; and *Plagal* when the fourth chord is followed by the first. This is commonly known as the '*Amen cadence*', and is used in Christian religious services.

Cadenza

The often florid **solo** section of a piece of music is called a **cadenza**. Throughout the **Baroque** era this would have been **improvised** to give the performers a chance to show off their talents. Throughout the classical era, **composers** often doubted or mistrusted the ability of the performers to improvise well and started to write out in full their intentions for the solo.

Suggested listening:
Mozart, flute concertos.

Canon

A **canon** (also known as a round) is when a piece of music is **repeated** by groups of performers, with each group overlapping the previous group. There can be a variable amount of parts, though up to four is most common. An example of this is the song *London's Burning*:

1	2	3	4
London's burning, London's burning, Call the engine, Call the engine, FIRE FIRE. Pour on water, Pour on water . . .	London's burning, London's burning, Call the engine, Call the engine, FIRE FIRE. Pour on water, Pour on water . . .	London's burning, London's burning, Call the engine, Call the engine, FIRE FIRE. Pour on water, Pour on water . . .	London's burning, London's burning, Call the engine, Call the engine, FIRE FIRE. Pour on water, Pour on water . . .

Cantabile

Cantabile is an Italian term meaning 'in a singing style' and is used to describe how the piece of music should be played or sung. This in turn means that the **melody** or tune should be performed smoothly and brought out.

Carol

The traditionally seasonal religious **songs** we hear around Christmas time such as *The First Noel, Away in a Manger* and *Ding Dong Merrily on High* are called **carols**.

One of the oldest English carols is *The Boar's Head Carol* which was first printed in 1521. Since the 18th Century in England, groups of singers have sung door-to-door as a money raising venture.

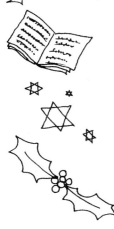

Cello

The **cello** (also known as *violoncello*) is the second largest **instrument** in the **strings** section of the **orchestra** and is made of wood. It is played between the knees in a seated position and has four strings, each tuned to an **interval** of a fifth.

The cello is essentially a large shaped hollow box with a neck, attached across which are stretched strings of different thickness. The strings are attached by a series of pegs which are used for tuning, and a **bridge** raises the strings from the wooden frame.

The strings on a cello can be plucked (*pizzicato*) or played with a bow (*arco*). **Chords** are also possible by playing more than one string at a time. This is also known as *double stopping*.

Suggested listening:
Elgar, *Cello Concerto*

Chamber Music

Originally **chamber music** was a term used to describe music not intended to be played in a church, a concert hall or public recital. The word has since lost this meaning and is now used to describe instrumental music on a small scale, including **solo** performances with **accompaniment**.

The term now encompasses **quartets, trios** and **quintets,** as well as orchestral pieces written for small **orchestras** such as those used in **concerto** grossos.

Suggested listening:
Bach, *Brandenburg Concertos*

Choir

The word **choir** has two meanings. Firstly it is a term used to describe a part of a cathedral (the *chancel* in a church); secondly (and more commonly), it is a term to describe a group of singers.

The latter is a broader term which has many subdivisions, including *mixed choir* (also known as a *chorus*) – consisting of male and female **voices**, *male voice choir* – using only male voices and popularised in Wales, and *barbershop choirs* – originally formed by barbers as a means of entertaining customers and passing the time. The barbershop choir is an **a capella ensemble**.

Suggested listening:
Verdi, *Requiem*
Carl Orff, 'O Fortuna', *Carmina Burana*

Chord

More than one **note** played at the same time is described as a **chord**.

This can be any combination of notes, though specific names have been given to certain combinations. For example, a common chord is when the first, third and fifth note of a **scale**, in a given **key**, are played at the same time. In the key of C major, these notes would be C, E and G.

G

E

C

Chromatic

Notes which move by the nearest step are called **chromatic**. Each of these move by way of an **interval** of a *semitone*.

If you look at a **piano keyboard** you will see white and black notes. If you played each of these in turn you would be playing a chromatic **scale**.

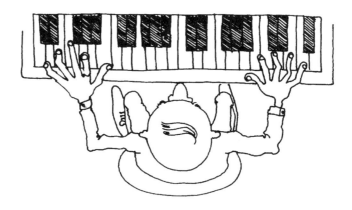

Clarinet

The **clarinet** is a member of the **woodwind** section of the **orchestra**. Traditionally they were made of wood, but have since been made from plastic and ebonite.

The clarinet is a cylindrical tube played by a single **reed** which, when blown, vibrates against the *mouthpiece* to produce the sound. The most common clarinet is called the *clarinet in B♭* because it is tuned to that **key**. Orchestral music often demands not only the B♭ clarinet but a clarinet in A, which is just a little longer. E♭ (smaller), *alto*, **bass** and *contrabass* clarinets (made from metal) are also widely used in larger **ensemble** music. The clarinet is used mainly as an **orchestral** or solo **instrument**, though it has been used quite extensively in **jazz** music.

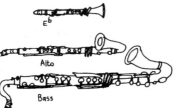

Suggested listening:
Mozart, *Clarinet Concerto*
Sid Philips, *Clarinet Marmalade*

Clefs

The symbol present at the beginning of a piece of music which is written in **stave notation** is called a **clef**. Each represents the **pitch** at which the music is written. There are four clefs:

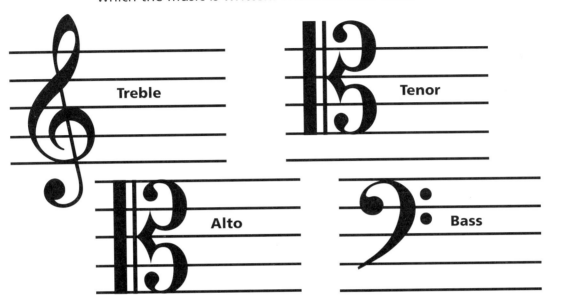

Treble

Tenor

Alto

Bass

Coda

A **coda** is a short section of music which is used to finish a piece. A **composer** will often use a coda to finish the piece as a means of making the music seem to have a greater sense of finality. A coda in western notation is signified by the sign ⊕.

Composer

The person responsible for creating a piece of music (**composition**) is called a **composer**.

Composition

Any piece of music that is made up from scratch is called a **composition**. This is regardless of how complicated or simple, easy or hard the piece is. The person creating the music is called a **composer**.

Crescendo

When a piece of music gradually becomes louder there is said to be a **crescendo**. When this is written on notation it is signified by a sign (<) or by the word *cresc*.

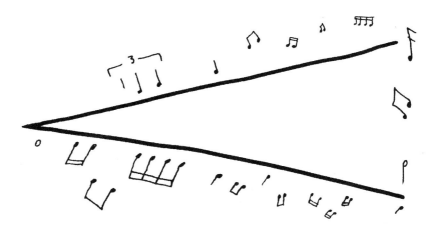

Crotchet

A **crotchet** is also referred to as a *quarter-note* as it is a quarter in value to a whole **note** or **semibreve**. When the **time signature** is 4/4 a crotchet would be worth one **beat**.

Concert

A **concert** is an event in which musicians perform to other people. This can range from a small informal event such as a school pupil playing to relatives at a family get-together, to a huge **rock** concert such as *Live Aid* in 1985, when a large number of **bands** played for famine relief at Wembley Stadium in front of a packed arena and the concert was transmitted to the world by television.

Concerto

The **concerto** is a piece of music divided into three sections (**movements**) for a **solo instrument** and **orchestra**. Most concertos follow a similar format of the order of movements: the first is of a moderate speed, the second slow and the third fast.

A forerunner of the concerto was the *concerto grosso*. This followed a similar format, but instead of the solo instrument there was a small group of instrumentalists. This group was called the *concertino* and the larger group was referred to as the *ripieno*. Some of the most famous concerto grosso are the *Brandenburg Concertos* of JS Bach.

Suggested listening:
Haydn, *Concerto Grosso*
Dvorak, *Cello Concerto*

Conductor

The person who controls and directs an **ensemble** or group of musicians, such as an **orchestra**, is called a **conductor**. This person would normally take control of practices (rehearsals) too.

In the 17th Century, groups were conducted by the person playing the **harpsichord**, though more commonly today we recognise the conductor as being the person who stands in front of an **orchestra** waving a thin white stick or *baton*.

Counterpoint

The technique of individual lines of music being woven together is called **counterpoint**. These lines go together to create a **harmony**. A **canon** is an exact form of counterpoint.

A most important style of counterpoint is *imitation*. This is when one **voice** (or **instrument**) imitates, but does not copy, another voice. The two lines sound good together, and though one line is by no means supporting or accompanying the other, each line is equally important.

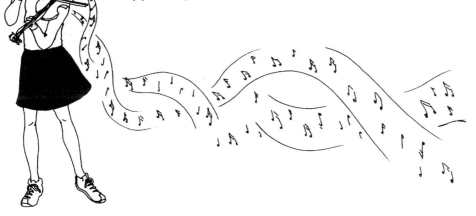

Cymbals

Cymbals look like big metal dishes. Orchestral cymbals have straps connected to the centre of the dish, and are held one in each hand so that they can be played by 'crashing' them together. Small cymbals are also used as part of a drum kit. These are known as 'high hats', and are played by using a foot pedal which crashes them together. Single cymbals can be struck with beaters or drum sticks.

Da Capo or D.C.

This is a musical term which means 'go back to the beginning'. If a **composer** wishes to have the first section of a piece repeated after the musicians have reached the end then he/she will use this device. A performer will continue through the music until the word *fine* (meaning end). Sometimes these directions are accompanied by a direction to go to **coda**.

Dal Segno

This musical term means 'go back to the sign'. The sign for dal segno is 𝄋. A **composer** will use a **dal segno** if he or she wishes the performer to repeat a section of music (though one that does not start at the beginning). A performer will continue through the music until the word *fine* (meaning end) or until the pause sign ⌢. Sometimes these directions are accompanied by a direction to go to **coda**.

Degrees of scales

Each **note** in a **scale** has a name which represents its position whatever scale it is. There are eight degrees, which are called:

1st: Tonic
2nd: Supertonic
3rd: Mediant
4th: Subdominant
5th: Dominant
6th: Submediant
7th: Leading note
8th: Tonic (octave)

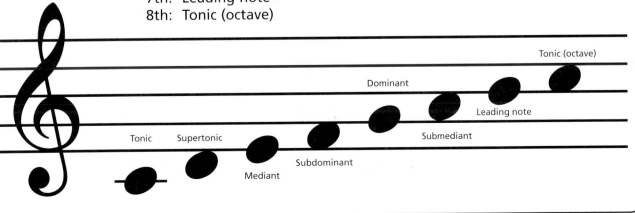

Didjeridu

The **didjeridu** is an instrument originally played by the Aborigines of Australia, as a means of communication as well as for pleasure. It is a long, cylindrical tube, which the player 'buzzes' down, changing the **pitch** by moving the mouth or cheeks. To keep the sound going continuously, the performer must breathe in at the same time as blowing out (this is called circular breathing).

Diminuendo

The Italian word **diminuendo** means gradually getting quieter. It is signified by a sign > or by the shortened version *dim*.

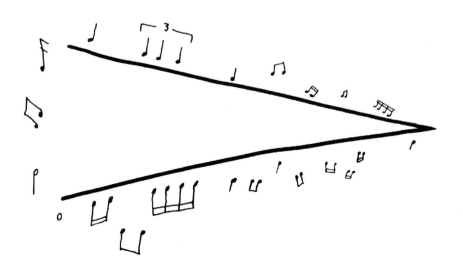

Double bass

The largest member of the **string** family is called the **double bass** (or sometimes *contra bass*). The player stands or sits on a high stool to play the instrument. It is made from wood and has four strings (very occasionally five), each *tuned* at the **interval** of a fourth. The strings are connected by *pegs* at the top of the neck which are tightened or loosened for tuning purposes. These strings are raised from the wooden frame by means of a thinner piece of wood called a **bridge**. The strings can be plucked (*pizzicato*) or played with a bow (*arco*).

As the instrument is so large, the **pitch** is very low. It is used extensively in **orchestras** (very often doubling the **cello** lines) and in **jazz** music where it is part of the **rhythm** section.

Suggested listening:
Saint-Saëns, The Elephant from *Carnival of the Animals*

Drone

A **drone** is a continuous sound.

The underlying sound made from **bagpipes** is a drone. Drones are also quite common in Indian music.

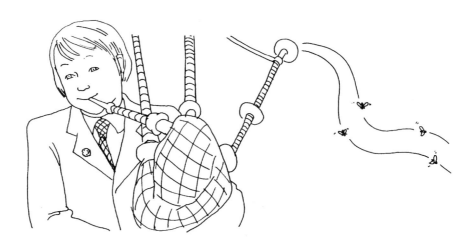

Drums

There are many types and sizes of **drum**, though basically they are cylindrical tubes with a tightened *skin* on the end. They are mainly played with sticks, though drums such as *conga* and *bongo* drums are played with the hands. Drums are members of the **percussion** section.

The drum kit is a selection of drums including a *snare*, **bass** and *tom-toms*, which are played in combination with *cymbals* by one person.

Duet

The combination of two performers, or a **composition** for such, is called a **duet** (also known as *duo*). This can be with or without an **accompaniment**.

Suggested listening:
Vivaldi, *Concerto in G minor for 2 cellos and orchestra RV.531*
Franz Doppler, *Andante and Rondo Op. 25 for two flutes and piano*

Dynamics

The word used to describe the *volume* in music is called **dynamics**.

The main words used in music to indicate the volume at which it should be played are:

term	abbreviation	meaning
fortissimo	*ff*	very loud
forte	*f*	loud
mezzo forte	*mf*	moderately loud
mezzo piano	*mp*	moderately quiet
piano	*p*	quiet
pianissimo	*pp*	very quiet
crescendo	*cresc* <	gradually getting louder
diminuendo	*dim* >	gradually getting quieter

Echo

If you were to go into a cave and shout 'hello' you would hear a repeat or many repeats of your **voice**. This is called an **echo**.

Just as when you look in a mirror you see a reflection of yourself, sound is *reflected* by walls and surfaces. The echo (or reflected sound) achieved will depend on the materials, size, shape and volume.

The **Symphony** Hall in Birmingham has been specially designed with a movable ceiling in order for varying acoustics (amounts of echo) to be achieved. This makes it one of the leading concert halls in the country.

Encore

When a performance is over, the audience often clap and cheer for the performer(s) to return to the stage and play another piece. When they do this is called an **encore**. The word is taken from the French word meaning 'again'.

Ensemble

1. A group of performers is called an **ensemble**. This can be any size of group and any combination of **instruments**.

2. The quality of *coordination* within a group of performers is often referred to as the **ensemble**.

Euphonium

The **euphonium** is a **brass instrument** which looks like and is made like a small **tuba**.

It is mainly used as an **ensemble** instrument in wind and **brass bands**, and little **solo** music has been written for it. It is rarely used in **orchestral** music, though the **composer** Holst used it in his suite *The Planets*.

Suggested listening:
Holst, Mars from *The Planets*

Figured bass

Figured bass was used mainly in the **Baroque** era to show the **harmony** (or inner part) of an **accompaniment**. A **composer** would write a melody and bass line, under which would appear numbers such as $\frac{6}{4}$ or $\frac{5}{3}$. These numbers are the **figured bass**.

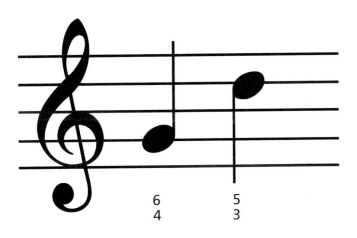

Flute

The **flute** is a member of the **woodwind** family and is commonly today made from silver, though originally it would have been made from wood.

It is a cylindrical tube, stopped at one end by a cork, with finger **keys** and a mouth hole. It is played *transversely* (sideways to the right) by blowing across the hole. By closing the keys, a player makes the tube longer or shorter, which in turn makes the **pitch** higher or lower.

The flute family consists of the most common or **concert** flute, the *piccolo*, which is smaller, and the *alto* and **bass** flutes which are larger.

Suggested listening:
Dave Valentin, *Red Sun*
James Galway, *The Man with the Golden Flute*

Form

The way in which a piece of music is organised is called the **form**. There are four traditionally used forms, each of which are used as a *structure* for the music regardless of how complex or simple the material is. (These letters refer to music ideas or subjects.)

Term	Structure of tunes						
Binary	A				B		
Ternary	A			B			A
Sonata		AB		A/B		AB	
		(Exposition		Development		Recapitulation)	
Rondo		A	B	A	C	A	D	A etc.

Gamelan

Gamelan is a style of music which comes from Indonesia. The **gamelan orchestra** is made up of a variety of gongs and drums. The music is highly organised into patterns.

Glissando

A *slide* between two or more **notes**, up or down, is called a **glissando**. A **piano** player running a thumb over all the white notes would produce a glissando. A *true* glissando, however, will incorporate all the notes of a **chromatic** scale.

If you can imagine that a staircase were all musical notes and you slid down them, it would produce the effect of a glissando.

Suggested listening:
Gershwin, *Rhapsody in Blue* (opening clarinet)

Ground Bass

A **bass** line which is repeated many times is called a **ground bass** (also known as a *passacaglia*). Over this repeated **theme** is a tune which changes and develops.

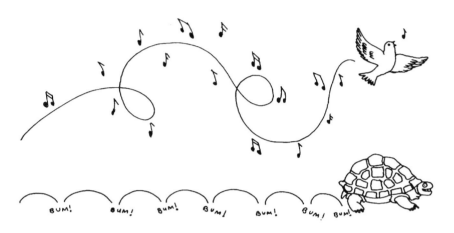

Suggested listening:
Theme music to *Mission Impossible*

Guitar

The traditional **acoustic guitar** is made with a resonating wooden *frame* and a *neck* along which six **strings** are stretched and adjusted by *pegs* at the end. It is played by *plucking* the strings either with fingers or a *plectrum* (a small hard device) ,or by *strumming*.

The development of popular music in the 1940s and 1950s gave rise to the *electric guitar* which is amplified using electricity and has a solid body. An electric guitar that has a *sound box* (ie, hollow) is known as a semi-acoustic.

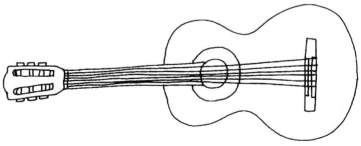

Suggested listening:
Rodrigo, *Guitar Concerto*
Jimi Hendrix, *Electric Ladyland*

Harmonica

A **harmonica** (also known as a mouth organ) is a small narrow box which encloses a number of small metal **reeds** of varying lengths. When blown, these reeds *vibrate* to create the sound. It was first invented in the 1830s and is commonly used in **blues** music.

Suggested listening:
Eric Clapton, *From the Cradle to the Grave*

Harmonics

When a note or *tone* is produced by a *vibration*, whether on a **string** or wind **instrument**, the sounds created are called **harmonics**.

Some **instruments**, such as the natural **trumpet** (which is straight and has no *valves*) were only able to produce harmonics, the **notes** of which were dependent on the length of the tube.

Suggested listening:
The last post – all notes of which use only the harmonic series.

Harmony

The mixture of **notes** to create **chords** and their relationship to each other is called **harmony**.

If you imagine a tune (*melody*) being the icing for a cake, the harmony would be the cake itself on which the icing can be supported.

Harp

The **harp** is an is an open-framed **instrument** with **strings** stretched over it in different lengths. These strings are played by the fingers.

The modern orchestral harp has seven *pedals*, each of which have two notches. These are depressed to enable the performer to change the length of the strings, thus changing the **key** in which to play. The shorter the strings, the higher the **pitch**. The longer the strings, the lower the pitch.

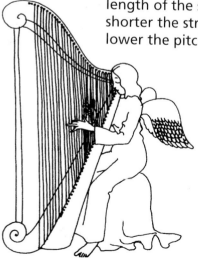

Suggested listening:
Mozart, *Flute and Harp Concerto*

Harpsichord

The predecessor to the **piano** was the **harpsichord**. The design looks similar, though the ways in which each produces **notes** is different. Notes on the harpsichord are produced when the **keys** are depressed, which in turn plucks the **strings** inside the frame. This means that regardless of how hard the keys are pressed, the resulting sound is of the same *volume*. As the sound is short, music written for harpsichord tends to be fast and *florid*.

The harpsichord was used mainly as an **accompanying instrument**, or one to direct **ensembles** such as that used in **concerto grosso**.

Suggested listening:
Vivaldi, Second movement, 'Autumn', from *The Four Seasons*

Horn

Although the **horn** is often called the *French horn*, it actually originated in Germany. It is a member of the **brass** family and is notably one of the hardest **instruments** to learn.

The French horn is made from a coiled brass tube with a flared opening (*bell*) at one end, where the performer inserts his/her hand. A system of *valves* enables the player to make the long tube shorter by degrees, thus enabling the player, in combination with lip pressure, to play different **notes**.

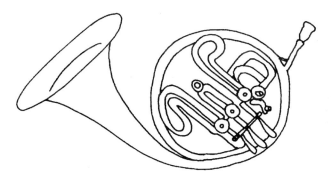

Suggested listening:
Mozart, *Horn Concerto*

Improvisation

When performers makes up music as they go along, they are *improvising*.

There are often guidelines to an **improvisation**. For example, in **jazz** improvisation performers will use the **chords** they are playing over as a guide to what **notes** they feel will sound good. In **baroque concertos**, performers were given the chance to play an improvisation near the end of each **movement** (cadenza). The *structure* for this, however, was still set and involved using notes only from relative **keys**.

Instruments

The devices used by musicians to create music are called **instruments**. Different types of instruments include **strings**, **brass**, wind (including **woodwind**) and **percussion**.

Interval

The distance between one **note** and another is called an **interval**.

The size of the distance is described by a number and a **key** reference. For example, from C to E is described as being a *major 3rd* because in the key of C major the note E is a third (three notes) away from C.

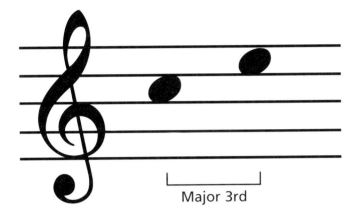

Major 3rd

Jam session

An informal *performance* which is usually open for anyone to join in is called a **jam session**. This usually comes in the form of musicians **improvising** and is common in **jazz** music.

Jazz

Jazz is a style of music which originated in New Orleans in the late 19th Century. Its development was due to a mixture of influences coming together in what was a centre for commercial business. The *Dixieland* **band** became established, using **instruments** from the white military bands and playing a form of the then developed **blues** and folk music.

As musicians travelled north, the Dixieland music met a greater number of influences and developed and evolved into a vast range of styles which are encompassed under the jazz title, such as *Be-bop* and *Swing*.

Suggested listening:
King Oliver's Creole Jazz Band
Charlie Parker
Duke Ellington

Key

1. The **key** of a piece of music is the association it has to a set group (**scale**) of notes. The *key signature* tells the performer what key the piece is in, and is always situated at the beginning of the **stave** after the **clef**. Each *major* scale has a relative *minor*. The diagram below shows all the keys in music.

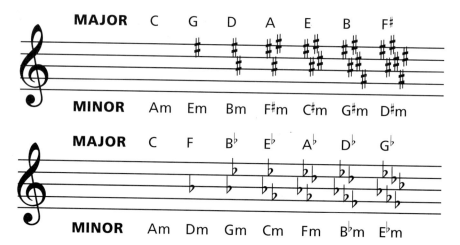

MAJOR	C	G	D	A	E	B	F♯
MINOR	Am	Em	Bm	F♯m	C♯m	G♯m	D♯m
MAJOR	C	F	B♭	E♭	A♭	D♭	G♭
MINOR	Am	Dm	Gm	Cm	Fm	B♭m	E♭m

2. The mechanism on **instruments** which, when depressed or released, changes the **notes**.

Keyboard

1. The group name for **instruments** such as the **piano** and **harpsichord**, which are played with two hands using a set structure of **keys**, is **keyboard**.

2. The *electric keyboard* has become an integral part of **pop bands**, and throughout its development has become increasingly able to imitate other instruments.

Suggested listening:
Chic Corea, *Electric band*

Largo

Largo is an Italian **tempo** (speed) marking meaning the music should be played very slowly and grandly.

Leger lines

The extra lines placed above or below a **stave** of music are called **leger lines**. These are used to accommodate the **notes** which are too high or low for the **stave**.

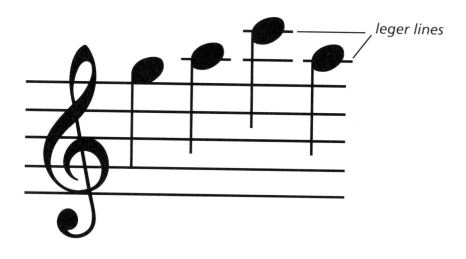

leger lines

Lento

Lento is an Italian **tempo** (speed) marking meaning the music should be played slowly.

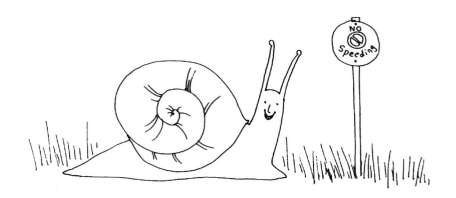

Lute

The **lute** was a predecessor to the **guitar**, but was more pear-like in shape. It was used as an **instrument** for entertainment in the Medieval and Renaissance periods, when lute players would often walk around their audience.

Suggested listening:
The Protheus ensemble, *Sweet love doth now invite*

Maestro

This word comes from the Italian *maestro di capella*, who was the director of a music establishment. It is now used, however, to stand for a master or teacher of music who is held in high esteem.

Mass

Since the 15th Century the **mass** has been an important form of sacred (religious) music in the Roman Catholic church. The music for the mass was divided into five **movements**: *Kyrie, Gloria in excelsis, Credo, Sanctus, Benedictus*, and *Agnus Dei*.

The *Requiem mass* is a mass for the dead. Many **composers** writing Requiem masses have expanded on the basic five-movement structure and have created highly dramatic and passionate works of music.

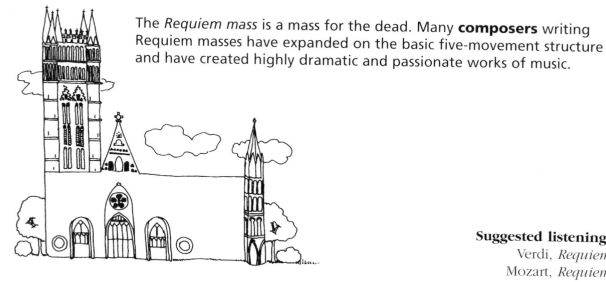

Suggested listening:
Verdi, *Requiem*
Mozart, *Requiem*

Melody

The *tune* in a piece of music is called the **melody**. The melody is usually **accompanied** by some **harmony**.

Metronome

A **metronome** is a device which gives a regular click and is used to set the speed of a **composition** or piece of music.

At the beginning of a piece of music there is often a direction of **tempo** (speed) in the form of '♩ = 60'. This means that there should be 60 **crotchet beats** per minute.

When this direction is accompanied by the letters M.M. it refers to the inventor Maelzel, who introduced the clockwork metronome.

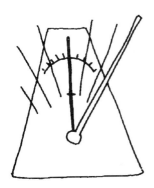

Minim

A **minim** is sometimes referred to as a half **note** as it is half the value of a whole note or **semibreve**. When the **time signature** of a piece of music is 4/4 a minim would be worth two **beats**.

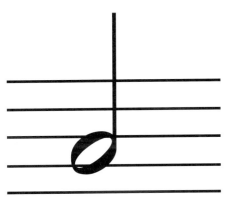

Moderato

Moderato is a **tempo** (speed) direction meaning that the music should be played at a moderate speed.

Modes

Modes are groups of **notes** which preceded **scales**. As with *major* and *minor* **scales**, modes used the spacing of **tones** or **semitones** between each note in a structured form. The names of the modes changed throughout the development of music, but the main six are: *Dorian, Phrygian, Lydian, Mixolydian, Aeolian* and *Ionian*.

Modes were used extensively in medieval **compositions**, but are also used sometimes by **jazz** musicians for their **improvisations**.

Modulation

Within a piece of music the **key** may change. This is called a **modulation**.

The most natural-sounding modulations are those that go to a *relative* key (see **key signatures**). For example, a change from C major to A minor or C major to G major are modulations used extensively in Western music, including **pop** music.

Movement

Large pieces of music such as **symphonies** are divided into smaller sections. These sections are called **movements**.

Each movement can be heard independently from the others and can be considered an individual piece. It is necessary, however, for movements within a larger work to combine effectively and still be *contrasting*.

Suggested listening:
Beethoven, *Moonlight Sonata – movement No 1*
Brahms, *Symphony No 4*

Mutes

The devices used to partially silence or *muffle* the sound of an **instrument** are called **mutes**.

Mutes are used on **stringed** instruments in the form of a *clamp* which is attached to the **bridge**; on **brass** instruments in the form of *cones* which are inserted into the bell; and on **drums** in the form of a *cloth* placed over the skin. Soft sticks can also be used to soften the sound on drums.

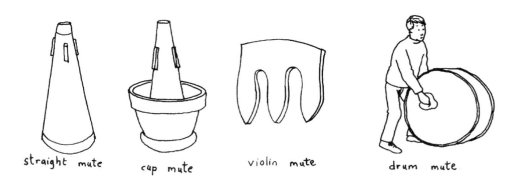

straight mute   cup mute   violin mute   drum mute

Nocturne

A **nocturne** is a piece of music which suggests night-time. It is usually written in three sections (*ternary* **form**) and evokes the stillness and calmness of night.

Suggested listening:
Chopin, *Nocturnes*

Notation

The means by which music is written down is called **notation**.

This can be in the form of letters of the alphabet or, more traditionally, by means of the **stave**. This is called stave **notation**. Each line and space of the stave represents the different **notes**, and **leger lines** are used for the more extreme notes. The diagram below shows the stave and letter name notation of notes on the *Treble* stave. Some modern (contemporary) music is notated in the form of graphs and is referred to as graphic notation.

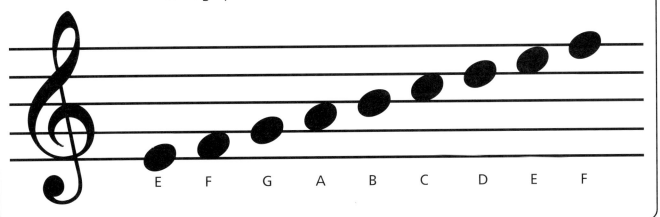

E F G A B C D E F

Note

A **note** is the name given to a written *sign* or *sound* which represents its **pitch** and length.

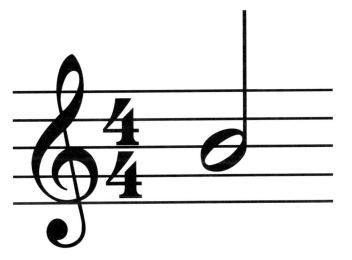

*B Minim = the note B lasts for two **beats***

Oboe

The **oboe** is a double **reed instrument** of the **woodwind** family. It was originally made from wood, though more recently from plastic. The sound is produced by blowing through the reeds into the *bore*, which has a combination of **keys** and finger holes. The different **notes** are made by moving the fingers over the holes and depressing the keys.

The larger version of the oboe is called the *Cor Anglais* or English horn. It is not known why, as it is neither a horn nor English.

Suggested listening:
Vivaldi, *Oboe Concertos*

Ocarina

An **ocarina** is a small egg-shaped wind **instrument** made from earthenware or metal. It is played by blowing through the mouth hole and moving fingers over the remaining holes in order to change **notes**.

It is not a widely used instrument nowadays.

Octave

The gap, or distance, between a note, for example, C, and the next C eight notes higher or lower is called an **octave**. The distance can be measured from high to low or from low to high.

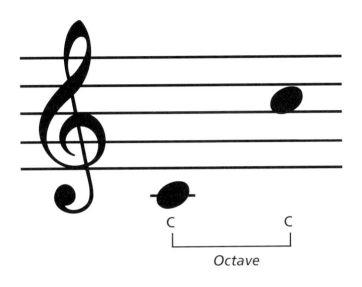

C   C

Octave

Octet

The combination of eight performers, or a piece of music for such, is called an **octet**.

The standard combination for a **string** octet is four **violins**, two **violas** and two **cellos**.

Many popular pieces of music are written for eight of the same **instruments**.

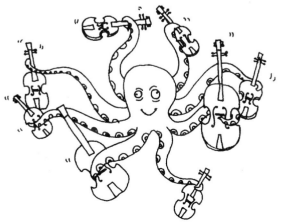

Opera

When a drama is set to music in its entirety, the result is called an **opera**. This consists of **solo**ists, chorus and **orchestral** music joined into a larger piece of work.

Operas are written for performance on stage with no spoken words (dialogue). The form came into being in the 1600s in Italy, where it was performed for small audiences of aristocrats, and has been developed ever since.

In modern times, smaller scale operas or those with a light-hearted feel are called *operettas*.

Suggested listening:
Verdi, *Aida*
Gilbert and Sullivan, music from operettas

Orchestra

A group of instrumentalists can be called an **orchestra.** The standard group, or most modern, has five sections of **instruments**: **woodwind, brass, string** and **percussion**.

The diagram below shows the way a standard orchestra would be seated in their instruments and sections.

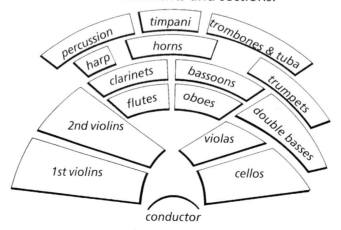

Suggested listening:
Britten, *Young Person's Guide to the Orchestra op. 34*

Organ

The **organ** is probably the largest of wind **instruments**, and although it uses air it is not blown – the air comes from *bellows* and *pumps*. It consists of three main sections: the *pipes*, which are graduated in size (relative to the **pitch**); the *stops*, which change the character of the sound when pressed or pulled; and the **keyboard** (of which there can be up to three, with an additional set of *pedals* played with the feet).

The pipes of organs in Christian churches became a focal point and were often very ornate.

Modern *electronic* organs have been developed (see **keyboards**) which can reproduce all the sounds on traditional organs within the compass of only one small box.

Suggested listening:
Bach, *Organ Concertos*
Original music from *The Blues Brothers*

Ornamentation

Within **stave notation**, some short *decorative* passages are added to some notes. The decorations which occur on or between the notes are referred to as **ornamentation**.

If you can imagine a rose in a vase being the centre of a flower arrangement, the foliage (green bits) surrounding it would be the ornamentation.

Suggested listening:
Vivaldi, *Flute Concertos*

Ostinato

A musical idea which is continuously repeated is called an **ostinato**. The ostinato can be in any part or on any **instrument** (thus a **ground bass** is also an ostinato, but restricted to the bass line of a tune). In **pop** or **rock** music, it is often called a *riff*.

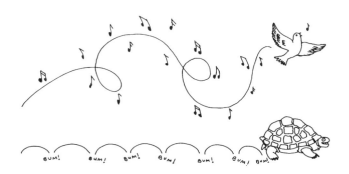

Suggested listening:
Mike Oldfield, *Tubular Bells*
Ravel, *Bolero*

Overture

An **overture** is a piece of *instrumental* music which was originally written as an introduction to an **opera** or *oratorio*. It can now, however, be used as an independent piece of music.

If you think of an opera being a meal, the overture would be the starter – an 'appetiser' of what is to come. However, the overture contains elements of what the rest of the musical 'meal' contains.

Suggested Listening:
Rossini, *William Tell Overture*

Pentatonic

A **pentatonic scale** is a group of five **notes**. If you were to play only the black notes on a **piano**, you would be playing a pentatonic scale.

The sounds that a pentatonic scale makes is very distinctive. A great deal of Chinese music uses only notes from this scale.

Notes of a pentatonic scale: C D E G A C

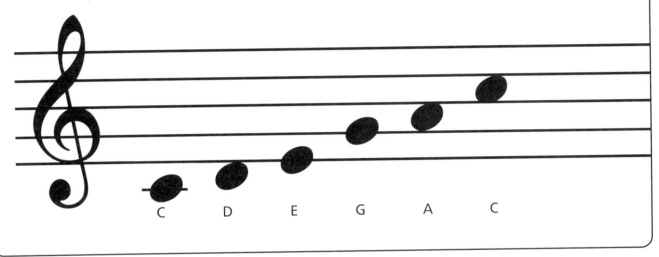

C   D   E   G   A   C

Percussion

Instruments which are sounded by being hit or shaken are called **percussion**. This group falls into two categories: *untuned* percussion, which provides mostly **rhythm** to a piece of music, and *tuned* percussion instruments which have definite **pitches**, such as the **xylophone**.

Phrase

When you sing or hum a **melody** it seems to fall into natural sections. These sections are called **phrases**. Phrases occur in all styles of music and are played on all **instruments**.

In the nursery rhyme *Twinkle Twinkle Little Star*, each line can be described as a phrase:

Twinkle Twinkle Little Star,
How I wonder what you are,
Up above the moon so bright,
Like a tiger in the night,
Twinkle Twinkle Little Star,
How I wonder what you are.

Piano

The **piano** (or pianoforte) is a large **instrument** which consists of a **keyboard**, a holding box, a frame and a set of **strings** of varying lengths. When the **keys** on the keyboard are pushed down they move *hammers* which hit the strings and create the sound. Depending on the intensity of the pressure used, the **dynamic** (volume) of the **notes** can be changed.

More recently, various kinds of *electric* pianos have been developed and are often used in **pop bands**.

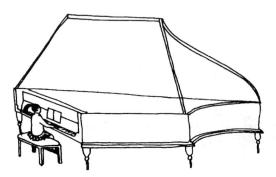

Suggested listening:
Joe Sample, *Roles*
Rachmaninov, *Piano Concerto No.2*

Pitch

1. The distinction between high and low **notes** in music is called **pitch**. If all music could be represented on a ladder, the top rungs would be high notes and the bottom rungs the low notes.

2. The ability to stay in the same place on one note is described at staying at **pitch**; this is also referred to as 'staying in tune'.

Pop music

The term **pop** (originally short for popular) is a representative term for whatever music happens to be popular at any one time, although it is usually thought of as the music which is in the pop charts. It is a general term to describe the music of the most popular **bands** or **solo** artistes at any one time. There are many different kinds of related music, including *rock 'n' roll*, **rock music**, *reggae*, *soul*, *Motown*, *rap*, *dance music* and so on.

Suggested listening:
The Beatles
The Spice Girls

Prelude

A **prelude** is a piece of music which was originally composed to be played before another piece.

In the 19th Century, preludes were composed as self-contained pieces and were often written for **piano**.

Suggested listening:
Chopin, *Piano Preludes*

Presto

Presto is an Italian speed (**tempo**) marking which describes a piece of music to be played fast.

If musical terms were compared to animals, the term presto would be represented by the fastest land animal – the cheetah.

Quartet

Any group or composition for four performers is called a **quartet**.

The **string** quartet is a popular **ensemble** and consists of two **violins**, one **viola** and one **cello**.

Quaver

A **quaver** is also known as an eighth **note**, as it is an eighth of a whole note or **semibreve**. When the **time signature** is 4/4 a quaver would be worth half a **beat**.

one quaver   *two quavers*

Ragtime

Ragtime is a type of American popular music which came into being in the early 20th Century. Often played on the **piano**, it is characterised by the **syncopated** (off the **beat**) effect created by the **melody** (tune) and a striding movement of the left hand, which is often playing **octaves**.

Suggested listening:
Scott Joplin, *Maple Leaf Rag*, *The Entertainer*, etc.

Recorder

The **recorder** is a **woodwind instrument** like a **flute**, but the sound is more hollow and is produced by blowing through a slitted *mouthpiece*. It has a conical *bore* with eight finger holes. By moving the fingers over the holes in a set way, different **notes** are produced.

The recorder is a very popular instrument which is used extensively in junior schools.

Reeds

The thin cane or metal device used for many **instruments** is called a **reed**. There are *single reeds*, which are used on **clarinets** and **saxophones**, and *double reeds* which are used on **oboes** and **bassoons**.

The sound of reed instruments is produced by the reed vibrating either against another reed (as with **oboes** and **bassoons**) or against a fixed structure such as a mouthpiece (as with **clarinets** and **saxophones**).

To illustrate how a double reed works, get two thick blades of grass, hold them together between your thumbs and blow through the gap. The grass will vibrate and creates a high **pitched** sound.

Reggae

Reggae is a style of music which originated in the Caribbean island of Jamaica. It has a strong off-beat feel, which is usually played by the **guitar**. It also usually has a strong **bass guitar** line.

Rests

In written musical **notation**, silence is indicated by **rest** signs. These have individual symbols and last for a specific amount of time.

The diagram below shows the rests and their values when the **key signature** is 4/4:

Semibreve and whole bar rest

Minim rest

Crotchet rest   or

Quaver rest

Semiquaver rest

Rhythm

When we hear a piece of music, we hear a structured variety of **notes**. The changeable lengths of these notes is the **rhythm**. The rhythm is held together and dependent on a regular **beat** or pulse.

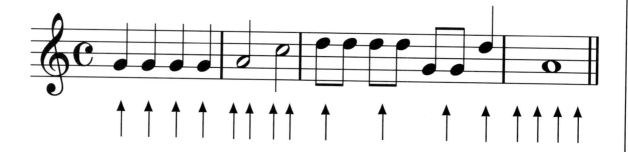

beat or pulse

Rock music

The early 1960s saw a change in style of music. At a time when communication and integration was a great developing aspect of music, influences were taken and **rock** music was born. Black musicians such as Otis Redding used the development of *electric* instruments to enhance their *gospel* based music, while white *country music* took on board the developments being made in the **jazz** style.

Rock can be seen as a representative of many other styles – for example **pop**, *rock 'n' roll*, *heavy metal*, *jungle*, *garage*, etc.

Suggested listening:
Elvis Presley, *Greatest Hits*
Queen, *Greatest Hits*

Romantic

At the turn of the 18th Century, many changes were happening in all the Arts. Literature and painting, as well as music, were all developing a deeper, more feeling aspect to them. This was to become referred to as the **romantic** era and takes music history through to the 20th Century.

Suggested listening:
Debussy, *La Mer*
Berlioz, *Symphonie fantastique*

Rubato

A **composer** will not always wish all of his/her music to be played strictly in time. For these sections, the composer will write the word **rubato**. Performers are then allowed to play the passage using their own discretion of how much or how little to slow down or speed up.

A rubato passage is only effective if it is carried out by a **soloist**.

Saxophone

The **saxophone** was designed by Belgian instrument maker Adolph Sax and came into existence in the 1840s. Since then it has been used extensively as an instrument in **jazz** and **pop** music. There are four types of saxophone: *soprano*, *alto*, *tenor* and *baritone*.

There is also a **bass** saxophone, though this is rarely used.

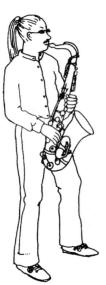

Suggested listening:
Charlie Parker
Dave Sanborne

Scales

Structured groups of **notes** which are played in order are called **scales**. The most common scales are *Major*, *Minor* and **Chromatic** scales. Scales can start on any note but have set *intervals* of notes.

Other scales used frequently in **compositions** are *Whole-tone* and **Pentatonic** Scales.

Scales are also representative notes of set **keys**.

Score

A **score** is a combination of all the parts of a piece of music. It is written down so that all the parts can be read at the same time. A **conductor** would use a score when directing an **orchestra**.

Semibreve

A **semibreve** is also known as a whole **note**. When the **time signature** is 4/4, a semibreve is worth four **beats**. As part of musical **notation** it looks like a circle on its own.

Sitar

A **sitar** is an **instrument** which is similar in principle to a **guitar**. It originates from the south of India and is most predominantly used in **classical** Indian music.

The sitar has seven **strings** on the outside and between nine and thirteen strings on the inside.

Solo

1. An instrumentalist or vocalist who performs on his or her own is doing a **solo**.

2. When there is an *instrumental* line of music which is most prominent it is called a **solo**.

3. **Improvisations** can also be called **solos**.

Song

A **song** is a poem or set of lyrics put to music in a vocal form. Most popular songs include a repeated section called a *chorus*, which is sung between each *verse*.

Suggested listening:
Top of the Pops

Stave

The five lines on which musical **notation** is written is called the **stave**. Each line and space of the stave represents an individual **note**, whether in *treble*, *tenor*, *alto* or **bass clef**.

Steel Pans

Steel pans originate from the Caribbean. They were made from oil cans, which were turned upside-down and then pounded into shape so that they made areas of different **pitches**. The performer uses beaters on the different areas to produce the tune. **Steel pans** come in a variety of sizes, which affect the **pitch**: the shorter the pan, the higher the **pitch**.

Suggested listening:
Bob Marley and the Wailers, *Iron, Lion, Zion*
Shabba Ranks, *Mr Loverman*

Strings

Instruments which use **strings** as a means of creating the music are called *stringed* instruments. These include the **harp**, **guitar**, **zither** and **sitar**.

The strings form the largest section of the **orchestra**. They are the **violins**, **viola**, **cello** and **double bass**. All of these orchestral instruments can be played *arco* (which means with a bow) or *pizzicato*, which means plucked.

Symphony

One of the most popular **forms** of music **composition** used in the **classical** period was the **symphony**. The word is derived from a Greek word meaning 'sounding together'.

Traditionally a symphony is a piece of music that has three distinct **movements** – a first of *moderate* speed, a second *slow* movement and a third *fast*. A fourth movement was sometimes introduced during the later classical and **Romantic** periods. Symphonies are played by **orchestras**.

Suggested listening:
Beethoven, *Symphony No 5*
Mahler, *Symphony No 2*

Syncopation

To change the **beat** or normal **accent** of a piece of music, so that strong beats become weak and weak beats become strong, is called **syncopation**.

Suggested listening:
Rumbas

Tabla

A **tabla** is a two-piece skinned **drum** which comes from the north of India. It is mainly used in Indian classical music.

Tabla are played with the fingers and usually from a seated position.

Tempo

The Italian word that describes the speed of a piece of music is **tempo**. The tempo marking is located at the top left hand corner of the music and is often accompanied by a **metronome** mark. Different tempos include **allegro**, **andante** and **largo**.

A composer wishing the music to gradually gain speed would use the word *accelerando*. Or, if the composer wants the music to gradually lose speed, the word *rallentando* is used.

Tie

In written musical **notation** a **tie** is a small curved line linking two **notes** of the same **pitch** together in order that the note is made longer. Most ties occur over a **bar** line, because it is impossible to create the desired length of note with a single note within the given time value of the bar.

For example:

1 A **crotchet** tied to another crotchet would be worth two beats.
2 A **semibreve** tied to a crotchet would be worth five beats.
3 A **quaver** tied to a crotchet would be worth one and a half beats.

Timbre

The quality of sound of an **instrument** or **voice**, or the combination of these, is called the **timbre**. Timbre is also referred to as *tone-colour*.

Time signature

In musical **notation** the **time signature** is located after the **key** signature at the beginning of the music. It tells the player how many **beats** there are in a **bar** and is written as one number on top of another.

The number on the top denotes how many beats there are in a bar, and the number on the bottom denotes what type of beat they are.

For example:

$\frac{4}{4}$ means there are 4 **crotchet** beats in a bar.

$\frac{2}{2}$ means there are 2 **minim** beats in a bar.

$\frac{6}{8}$ means there are 6 **quaver** beats in a bar.

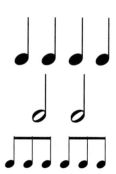

Tone

1. A sound which has a definite **pitch** and length can be referred to as a **tone**.

2. The distance of two semitones is called a **tone**.

3. The **timbre** or quality of sound is also referred to as **tone**.

Tonguing

When playing a **woodwind** or **brass instrument**, it is essential that the beginning of the **note** is clear and neat. Players, to achieve this, will use the tongue to start the note by means of a 'tu' sound. To achieve varying speeds, **accents** or style of note, a player may use differing styles of **tonguing**. There are four main ways of doing this:

1. *Single* tonguing, when the performer will play 'tu' 'tu' 'tu'.

2. *Double* tonguing, when the performer plays 'tu' followed by a 'ku' created by the tongue within the mouth.

3. *Triple* tonguing when the performer plays 'tu' followed by 'ku' followed by 'tu' again.

4. *Flutter* tonguing, when the performer blows the note whilst rolling their tongue as you would when you roll your r's.

Transpose

When you change the **pitch** of piece of music from its original at a fixed **interval** (distance), you **transpose** it.

Some **instruments**, such as the **clarinet** and the **trumpet**, are referred to as *transposing* instruments. This is because they play in a different **key** to that of concert pitch, which is the key of C. Examples of instruments that play at concert pitch are the **piano** and the **flute**.

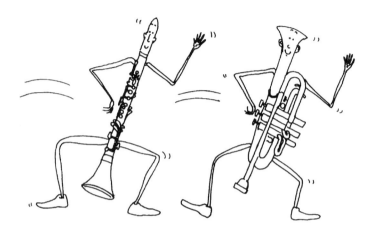

Trio

A group of three performers or a piece of music written for such a group is called a **trio**.

A standard **string** trio would consist of **violin**, **viola** and **cello**.

Trombone

The **trombone** is a member of the **brass** family. It evolved from an **instrument** called a *sackbut*. The sound is produced by blowing down the curved cylindrical tube, and the **notes** are changed by extending and retracting the *slide* and changing the lip pressure.

Trombones used to be made in three sizes – the **bass**, *alto* and *tenor*. The alto and tenor were joined by means of a *valve*, which enabled one trombone to encompass the range of the two.

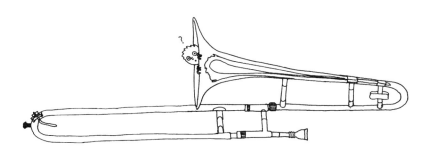

Trumpet

The **trumpet** is the highest **pitched instrument** in the **brass** family. The original (or 'natural') trumpet was a long cylindrical tube which played only a selection of **notes** based on the **harmonic** series. *Valves* were later added to the trumpet in and the tube curved round. The valves changed the length of the tubing and therefore enabled the player to play a wider selection of notes using varying lip pressures.

Suggested listening:
Miles Davis, *A Kind of Blue*
Haydn, *Trumpet Concerto*

Tuba

The largest of the **brass** section of **instruments** is the **tuba**. It is also the lowest in **pitch**. As with the **trumpet**, the tuba is constructed of a long cylindrical tube which is wrapped round on itself, with the *bell* at one end and the mouthpiece at the other. Sound is produced by blowing through the *mouthpiece*, and the sound is changed by lip pressure and use of the four *valves* which are played by the fingers.

Unison

When instrumentalists are playing or singing the same thing at the same time, they are said to be in **unison**.

Vibrato

Vibrato is when a **note** changes **pitch** rapidly.

For example, when an **instrument** is being played by blowing, vibrato is achieved by either lip pressure or control of the air. A **strings** player will move the fingers of the left hand to change pitch and create this effect. If you can imagine a sound as a jelly, wobbling the jelly would create the effect of vibrato.

Violin and Viola

The **violin** and **viola** are each basically a shaped hollow box with a *neck* attached, across which are stretched **strings** of different thickness. The strings are attached by a series of *pegs* which are used for tuning, and a **bridge** raises the strings from the box. Both instruments can be played by plucking the strings (*pizzicato*) or with a bow (*arco*).

The viola differs from the violin by being about six inches longer. This creates a lower **pitch**. The main use for the viola is as a middle accompanying **voice** to a string section.

Suggested listening:
Yehudi Menuhin
Brahms, *Violin Concerto*

Voices

The **voice** is one musical **instrument** that we all have. When we sing, folds of skin in our throat (vocal cords) vibrate and the cavities in our chest or head *resonate* to create the sound. By using muscles attached to these cavities, we automatically change the **pitch** or *syllable* of the notes.

In most *choral* music, the types of voice are arranged into order of **pitch**, e.g. *soprano*, *alto*, *tenor*, *baritone*, **bass**.

soprano   alto   tenor   bass

Woodwind

The **woodwind** section of the **orchestra** consists of the **flute, oboe, clarinet** and **bassoon**. It was so called because all of these **instruments** were traditionally made from wood and blown.

The introduction of the **saxophone** to the woodwind family in the 1840s became the exception, as it was never made from wood.

Xylophone

The **xylophone** is a tuned **percussion instrument** played with beaters. It is made from wooden blocks of different lengths which are arranged on a frame.

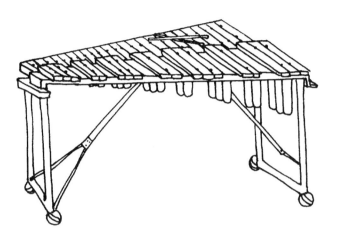

Zither

The **zither** is a **stringed instrument** made from a closed wooden box which has between 30 and 45 strings stretched over the surface. It is played by *plucking* the strings using a *plectrum* (a small piece of hard material) and stopping the strings over *frets* with the other hand. The zither originally came from Eastern Europe.